Triple J Publishing

SHORT-RUN BOOK PUBLISHING SPECIALIST

Book Publishing Guide For Authors

Triple J Publishing

Triple J Publishing

SHORT-RUN BOOK PUBLISHING SPECIALIST

Book Publishing Guide For Authors

Triple J Publishing
Sanford, NC

Book Publishing Guide For Authors
Copyright © 2011
Ophelia W. Livingston

THE HOLY BIBLE, NEW INTERNATIONAL VERSION®, NIV® Copyright © 1973, 1978, 1984, 2011 by Biblica, Inc.™ Used by permission. All rights reserved worldwide.

ISBN-13: 978-0-9840853-3-0
ISBN-10: 0-9840853-3-5

For additional copies of this book, contact *Triple J Publishing*.
Cover designed by Triple J Graphics
Edited by Barbara S. Keller

Triple J Publishing, Sanford, North Carolina
Printed in the United States of America
www.triplejpublishing.com
1-866-579-7475
Library of Congress Control Number: 2011932857

Email: triplejpublishing@gmail.com

Job Descriptions in Today's Ministry by Ophelia Livingston—Used with permission
Life Has Meaning by Regina Jenkins Emerson—Used with permission
All The Praise by Ophelia Livingston—Used with permission

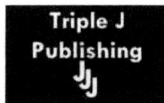

**Triple J
Publishing
JᴊJ**

Four Quotes to Inspire Writers

"Your attitude is everything. Believe in yourself and trust your material. To be a successful writer, write every single day, whether you feel like it or not. Never, never give up, and the world will reward you beyond your wildest dreams."
~Alex Haley

"A word is a bud attempting to become a twig. How can one not dream while writing? It is the pen which dreams. The blank page gives the right to dream."
~Gaston Bachelard

"Every accomplishment large and small begins with the same decision: I'll try."
~Ted Key

"One writes out of one thing only—one's own experience. Everything depends on how relentlessly one forces from the experience the last drop, sweet or bitter, it can possibly give."
~James Baldwin

〜〜〜 〜〜〜 〜〜〜 〜〜〜

Triple J Publishing frees authors to focus on what they do best: write. For one low fee, we will edit and typeset your book, design the cover, create the PDF file, provide at-cost printing, design a web site and a marketing plan. No other company provides an honest, reputable service like this.

Contents

Triple J Publishing

1-866-579-7475

triplejpublishing@gmail.com
www.triplejpublishing.com
Fax (919) 775-2365

150 N. Steele St, Suite 102
Sanford, NC 27330

Introduction

Triple J Publishing is a Christian company, dedicated to furthering the work of authors through the written word. It is our sincere understanding that God is the architect of all good things, including social media and technology. Using modern technology and collaborative partnership to its fullest, *Triple J Publishing* believes its directive is to produce high quality books at very affordable prices.

Traditional book publishers rarely look at an unsolicited manuscript by an unknown author. That does not necessarily mean the manuscript is unworthy of publication, but rather that it is not a manuscript guaranteed to sell in the large quantities that these publishers must mass produce. There are many potential books that have very specialized markets that can support hundreds of copies, but not thousands. *Triple J Publishing* has recognized the need and the potential ministry opportunity in this unfulfilled market niche. Specialized techniques, along with a skilled, dedicated, and committed staff have brought *Triple J Publishing* to the forefront of the short-run publishing marketplace.

Triple J Publishing understands the special needs of a successful book—whether a novel, children's book, non-fiction or special interest. *Triple J Publishing* gives specific advice garnered from our experience in publishing and selling books. We look at each book as unique—demanding individual tailored attention.

A good example of the need for professional, individual attention is an attractive book cover design. Many self-published books have an obvious self-published "hue" to them. You will not find that with our designs. No two books are ever the same. Book cover designs can become an emotional venture for the author. We take all of the emotions into account and try to produce the right cover design for your book, while at the same time staying within your budget.

Our publishing company will evaluate manuscript submissions according to editorial need, literary quality, theological soundness and topic interest. Under certain circumstances, it is possible that we will be unable to publish your manuscript. Triple J's editorial staff has the discretion to return your manuscript to protect the integrity of our company

Book Publishing Procedure

Step 1

Read this guide carefully. Accurate compliance with these guidelines will potentially lower your costs. Fill out the form at the end of this guide.

Step 2

Mail (CD or USB flash drive) or email (zipped PDF or MS Word) your manuscript in printed form to *Triple J Publishing* along with any cover sketches or ideas you have.

Step 3

We will carefully analyze your manuscript. Once approved, your manuscript is assigned for imprint. We typeset sample pages for you and draw up a publishing agreement list of all price details. At this point, you owe nothing! With your return of the signed agreement authorizing work to begin, however, we require 50% of the cost up front. *Triple J Publishing* accepts Visa, MasterCard, Discover and American Express for all payments.

Step 4

Triple J Publishing editors, typesetters, and graphic designers begin work. The author is consulted with regard to cover text, any missing ingredients, such as minor edits, major edits, ghost writing, photos, drawings, etc.

Step 5

Page proofs of the book and a color proof of the cover are sent to you, the author, for your approval. ISBN and bar code are secured and a copyright is recorded in the author's name.

Step 6

Along with your approval of the page proofs and color proof of the cover, we require the second installment of 25 percent of the balance. Occasionally, a second proof will be requested by the author. Subsequent proofs will be sent via e-mail in PDF format (soft copy). You may choose to have page proofs (hard copy) instead; however, this will incur a shipping charge. Final changes are made and with your approval, all changes are finalized. The final 25 percent installment of the payment is made.

Step 7

Upon final payment and book orders, books can be ordered and shipped to the designated address.

Publishing Services

Typesetting

Included with your publishing agreement will be sample pages typeset for your approval based on your choice of styles from the back of this guide. Upon receipt of your signed agreement, we typeset the remainder of the book. Provided the manuscript is on a USB flash drive or CD, typesetting is included in the printing price. If the manuscript is not supplied as a soft copy, a charge of $3 per page will be incurred.

Inside Cover Page

Provided the style is similar to the cover, this set-up is included in the printing cost.

ISBN & Bar Code

International Standard Book Number (ISBN) registration, as well as the corresponding bar code, is included in the printing cost. ISBN is a thirteen-digit number (it used to be ten-digits) that uniquely identifies books and book-like products published internationally. The purpose of the ISBN is to establish and identify one title or edition of a title from one specific publisher.

Copyright

The copyright notification is issued in the author's name; therefore, all rights belong to the author, not *Triple J*

Publishing. This is included in the printing cost. (For more details on copyright, please see page 29.)

LCCN

Libraries use the Library of Congress database as well as other databases to stay up-to-date on available titles. Make it easier for them to purchase your book by registering for a Library of Congress Control Number (LCCN), a unique identification number that the Library of Congress assigns and uses for cataloging and other book processing activities. We will complete an application for your LCCN on your behalf and submit it to the Library of Congress. You will receive your LCCN from us within 15 business days. To be considered for cataloging within the Library of Congress database, we will submit one copy of your book to the Library of Congress.

Paper

Books are usually printed on the same type paper on which this book is printed.

Perfect Binding

Binding with a flat spine is generally the preferred method and is included in the printing cost. For books with 50 pages or less, saddle-stapling is the default method of binding.

Saddle-Stapling Binding

Saddle-Stapling Binding is commonly used for small booklets, calendars, pocket-size address books, and some magazines. Several sheets of paper are folded (the fold becomes the spine of the booklet) and two or more staples are placed in the fold.

Proofreading

Triple J Publishing believes that all books need at least a basic proofreading, and it is included at a cost of $50-$75. This proofreading ensures consistent quality across all imprints and ensures your book will not be dismissed by readers or booksellers based on a previous bad experience. Proofreading corrects misspellings, punctuation errors and inconsistencies. It does not involve major rewriting of sentences. After our initial reading, we will indicate on the publishing agreement whether or not we suggest more thorough proofreading or editing for your manuscript. However, accepting the suggestion is solely the author's decision.

Editing

More than proofreading, editing includes the re-writing of sentences to improve readability, focus, and the author's story intent. The price varies according to the work requirement including a $100 set-up fee plus a range from $5.00 to $50.00 per page.

Cover Design

Triple J Publishing takes great pride in designing your book cover. The old saying still holds true today: most books are judged by their covers. The importance of a cover design should never be underestimated. Cover design is not included in the printing cost due to varying needs, details, images, and wants of each individual subject and author. We will provide a cost estimate on the publishing agreement subject to certain restrictions. Generally, the range is between $450-$700. Compare this to most graphic designers who will charge $700-$3000+ for cover designs. If the author has a budget he or she wishes to set, *Triple J Publishing* will abide by that budget and design accordingly.

UV Coating for Covers

The book you are holding has a UV-coated cover, which is a finish widely used for books. It both protects the cover from stains and markings and gives a brighter, glossy shine to the cover. This is highly recommended.

Photographs

All black/white photographs inside the book cost $12 each. Color photographs are substantially more expensive and will likely change the book production method. Please ask for more information if you are considering color photographs inside your book.

Photo Retouching/Photo Manipulation
These services are charged on a per-hour basis. Ask for a quotation on any retouching/manipulation you are considering.

Pictures, Diagrams, Illustrations
All are available at varying costs. Projects involving many illustrations or diagrams will be looked at individually. Supplied graphics, on USB flash drive or CD, are subject to a $12 layout charge per graphic. If supplied on CD, USB flash drive must have a minimum resolution of 300 dpi or better and should be in JPEG, BMP, or TIFF formats. Other formats may be acceptable. For more information, email *Triple J Publishing* at triplejpublishing@gmail.com or phone 1-866-579-7475.

Translation
Triple J Publishing can print books in almost any language. For information, email *Triple J Publishing* at triplejpublishing@gmail.com or phone 1-866-579-7475.

Shipping
Shipping costs are extra. The general range is $45-$65 per case of books depending on location and method of shipment. Shipping cost are calculated based on shipping one lot to one location. Multiple locations my incur additional cost.

Additional Services

Triple J Publishing provides many additional services related to printing, marketing, and distribution. The following is a sampling of what we offer at our usual competitive prices.

Graphic Design Services

Our skilled staff can create logos, letterhead, business cards, posters, labels, etc. for your promotional and business efforts. Contact us for price quotes.

Full-color Bookmarks

Full-color bookmarks are available for your marketing needs. Bookmarks are approximately 2" x 6", with full-color photo of the book and ordering information. Bookmarks are a valuable tool for increasing recognition in the marketplace.

Customized bookmarks are available at an additional cost.

Writing Services

Triple J Publishing writers can put together ad copies, promotional letters, or just anything else in a professional, effective manner. We provide manuscript critiques if you are unsure of whether you should proceed with publishing.

Grammatical Reference Section

Final typesetting and page layout will usually be done by *Triple J Publishing*. Careful observance of the following guidelines, however, will save considerable extra time and expense in preparing your manuscript for publication.

A. Manuscript Submission
Manuscripts should be submitted in the following formats. Sending an electronic copy is highly recommended.

1. Computer Disk (CD)
   a. CD in any major word processor or page layout program. PDF format is preferred. However, WordPerfect, Microsoft Word, or Microsoft Works, etc. is acceptable. Send TWO identical copies of each CD to minimize disk errors.

   b. We prefer the entire manuscript be sent as a single computer file; however, each chapter may be saved as a separate file if a list of file names is supplied in the order that they should appear in the book. **Do not save each page as a separate file.** If a separate file is used, please flow all text together, separating each chapter by means of triple line spacing and chapter headings. If a separate file is used for each chapter, label files in a clearly descriptive manner: e.g. CHAP1, CHAP 2, etc.

c. Manually type page numbers on your copy. Automatic page numbering is acceptable but not necessary.

d. Do not type words in "all capital letters", especially titles and subheadings.

2. USB Flash Drive
Same as the information for computer disk.

3. Hard Copy
   a. 8 ½" x 11" paper, single spaced, standard 1" margins, unjustified and ragged right margin.

   b. Pages should be numbered and/or individual chapters stapled together.

B. Spacing
   1. Use the <TAB KEY> to indent the first

line of each paragraph. Do not use the **<SPACE BAR>** to indent lines.

2. Headings and subheadings may be separated from the main body of the text with double line spacing.

3. Body text paragraphs should be separated from each other by a single line space bar only.

4. Block quotations (quotes which will be indented in the book) should be separated from the rest of the text with double line spacing before and after, using the regular page margins.

5. Sentences should be separated from each other by one space after a period, not two spaces.

C. Capitalization
Capitalize the first letter of the following words:
1. Proper nouns: e.g. Dr. Smith, Sanford.

2. Proper adjectives derived from proper nouns: e.g. American culture, Reformed tradition.

3. Nationalities and denominations: e.g. Indian, Mexican, Baptist, Presbyterian.

4. Languages: e.g. English, Spanish, German.

5. The pronoun *I*.

6. Titles: e.g. *Life Has Meaning, All The Praise*.

7. First word of a sentence.

8. Pronouns referring to God (He, Him, His, You, Your, One, Me, Mine, My, Son) may or may not be capitalized at your discretion, but be consistent throughout your document. Capitalization in Scripture quotations should be the same as in the version quoted, regardless of the pronoun capitalization in the remainder of the document.

NOTE: Capitalize **consistently**.

E.g. **C**hurch (the Body) or **c**hurch (the place); **K**ingdom (when referring to God's Kingdom) or kingdom (when referring to any other kingdom); **S**cripture(s); **b**iblical; **W**ord (when referring to the Bible).

D. Quotation Marks

Put double quotation marks around the following:

1. Titles of essays and articles.

2. Chapters and sections of books.

3. Titles of poems, short stories, television programs, and songs.
4. Mottoes and other familiar quotations.

5. Direct quotes.

NOTE: A quote within a quote should be set off with single quotation marks. A quote within a quote within a quote should be set off with double quotation marks, and so on.

Example: Jamie said, "James said 'hello' to me today!"

E. Italics

Italicize the following:

1. Titles of published books: e.g. *All The Praise*

2. Titles of pamphlets: e.g. *How to Fix Chip Cup,* periodicals, newspapers, reports, works of art, movies, long musical compositions, full length plays.

3. Foreign words and phrases: e.g. *bonjour.*

4. Words used as words or phrases: e.g. There is one *s* in the word *desert.*

5. Scripture verses may be put in italics rather than quotation marks if so desired: e.g. *Let everything that hath breath praise the Lord. Praise ye the Lord (Psalm 150:6).*

6. Words that are being emphasized.

NOTE: If possible, please do not use underline in place of *italics.*

F. Abbreviations

Where possible, avoid the use of abbreviations. However, the following abbreviations are commonly accepted:

1. Titles before and after proper nouns: e.g. Dr. James Livingston, M.D.

2. Dates and times: e.g. B.C., A.M.

3. Established organizations or agencies: e.g. FBI, NCAA, MLB.

4. Certain standard phrases used in reports and footnotes to save space and needless

repetition: e.g. (for example), etc. (etcetera), pp. (pages).

5. Books of the Bible:

Old Testament

Gen.	(Genesis)	Prov.	(Proverbs)
Exod.	(Exodus)	Eccl.	(Ecclesiastes)
Lev.	(Leviticus)	Song of Sol.	(Song of Solomon)
Num	(Numbers)	Isa.	(Isaiah)
Deut.	(Deuteronomy)	Jer.	(Jeremiah)
Josh .	(Joshua)	Hos.	(Hosea)
Judg.	(Judges)	Joel	(Joel)
Ruth	(Ruth)	Amos	(Amos)
1 Sam.	(1 Samuel)	Obad.	(Obadiah)
2 Sam.	(2 Samuel)	Jonah	(Jonah)
1 Kings	(1 Kings)	Micah	(Micah)
2 Kings	(2 Kings)	Nahum	(Nahum)
1 Chron.	(1 Chronicles)	Hab.	(Habakkuk)
2 Chron.	(2 Chronicles)	Zeph.	(Zephaniah)
Ezra	(Ezra)	Haggai	(Haggai)
Neh.	(Nehemiah)	Zech.	(Zechariah)
Esther	(Esther)	Mal.	(Malachi)
Lam.	(Lamentations)		
Ezek.	(Ezekiel)		
Dan.	(Daniel)		
Job	(Job)		
Ps.	(Psalms)		

New Testament

Matt.	(Matthew)	1 Tim.	(1 Timothy)
Mark	(Mark)	2 Tim	(2 Timothy)
Luke	(Luke)	Titus	(Titus)
John	(John)	Philem.	(Philemon)
Acts	(Acts)	Heb.	(Hebrews)
Rom.	(Romans)	Jas.	(James)
1 Cor.	(1 Corinthians)	1 Pet.	(1 Peter)
2 Cor.	(2 Corinthians)	2 Pet.	(2 Peter)
Gal.	(Galatians)	1 John	(1 John)
Eph.	(Ephesians)	2 John	(2 John)
Phil.	(Philippians)	3 John	(3 John)
Col.	(Colossians)	Jude	(Jude)
1 Thess.	(1 Thessalonians)	Rev.	(Revelation)
2 Thess.	(2 Thessalonians)		

NOTE: Use either full names of Bible books or abbreviations consistently (i.e. full names within a sentence, abbreviations in bracketed references).

G. Numbers

The following numbers must be written out in full:

1. Numbers at the beginning of sentences: e.g. Five hundred ten people attended the workshop.

2. Numbers less than one hundred (in non-scientific writing): e.g. The man had fifteen snakes cages in his apartment.

The following numbers must be given in figures rather than spelled out in full:

1. Measurement symbols: e.g. She ran the 5280 feet to the store rather than driving.

2. Times, dates, temperature, decimals, percentages, street addresses: 9:00 P.M.; June 1, 2011.

3. When outlining points, use a consistent numbering/lettering system: e.g.

    I.
      A.
        1.
        2.
          a.
          b.
            i.
            ii.

H. Punctuation

1. Use apostrophes correctly: e.g. girl's hair, teachers' lounge, men's dorm, ABC's can't.

NOTE: *it's* = it is; *its* is possessive.

2. Commas—use the following standard for consistency.

a. Main clauses, and/but/or main clause.
b. Main clauses, for/nor...
c. Subordinate clause, main clause.
d. Introductory word or phrase, main clause.
e. Word, word, and word...
f. Phrase, phrase, and phrase...

3. Semi-colons:
a. Main clause; main clause.
b. Main clause; so that/therefore, main clause.
c. Main clause; main clause; and the main clause...

4. Punctuation and Quotation marks
a. Periods and commas always go inside the quotation marks: e.g. After hearing the song "Amazing Grace," Janel was uplifted.

b. Other punctuation (?!) goes inside or outside the quotation marks, depending on what it belongs to: e.g. Jewel, you ever seen Law and Order"? "Of course I have!" she replied.

5. Where a Scripture reference concludes a quoted Bible verse, the period for the

sentence comes at the end of the Scripture reference: e.g. *Lift up your heads, O ye gates; even lift [them] up, ye everlasting doors; and the King of glory shall come in.* (Psalm 24:9, KJV).

6. Use an ellipsis (three periods) when omitting words in the middle of a quote; four dots at the end of a sentence: e.g. Acts 16: 14 says, *And a certain woman named Lydia, a seller of purple, of the city of Thyatira, ...whose heart the Lord opened, that she attended unto the things which were spoken of Paul.*

7. Type a dash as a double hyphen (--). This will convert into proper dashes during type-setting: e.g. I cannot believe Barbara dropped it—in the middle of the kitchen floor, of all places—and then left without cleaning it up!

   NOTE: Any words added to or changed in a quotation need to be enclosed in square brackets.

I. **Miscellaneous**

1. Make sure Scriptures quotations and references are accurate.

2. Indicate which Bible version(s) you are using. A copyright statement is required on the

copyright page. The following format should be used to reference the *main* version of Scripture that is used throughout the text:

3. Choose one version of the Bible for the majority of your scripture quotations and identify that version at the beginning of the manuscript; for example: "Bible verses are taken from the New King James Version (NKJV) unless otherwise noted."

4. Indent the citation within the body of the text. Place the citation between parentheses. Abbreviate the name of the book, then cite the chapter and verse, using numbers and separating them with a period.

5. Ezekiel saw "what seemed to be four living creatures," each with faces of a man, a lion, an ox, and an eagle (Ezek 1:5-10).

6. Use the standard abbreviation if you quote material from a different version of the Bible than you've cited as the main version used: (John 3:16, NIV).

7. Use a comma followed by a space when quoting citations from two or more verses that are not in sequential order: (John 3:16, 18).

8. Use an en-dash when quoting citations taken from three or more verses simultaneously: (John 3:16-18).

9. Use a semicolon when quoting separate citations taken from different chapters or books: (John 3:15, 17; 5:10) (John 3:15; Luke 11:4).

   All Scripture quotations, unless otherwise specified, are taken from the (cite the version) of the Bible. Copyright © ... Used by permission of ...)

   Check what wording is required in the specific Bible version(s) you are quoting from. These requirements can be found on the Bible's copyright page. **All Bible versions used must be indicated in your manuscript.**

eBook Conversion

The demand for this service is heavy so we are converting authors' books on a first-come, first-served basis. We provide formatting services for the Amazon Kindle and other eReaders. We provide files in .mobi format for Amazon and in .epub format for other distributors.

Formatting a book for eReaders is essentially a matter of converting the page layout files or PDFs into HTML and then tweaking that HTML so the final result looks good on Kindle devices. Simply contact us and send us your manuscript. We will do the rest. At the end you will receive your digital book in the following formats:

1. ePUB (iPad, Nook, eReader, and many more...)
2. .mobi (Kindle, MobiPocket)
3. PDF

Once we have your book converted, we will send you the files and, upon request, upload your book to the iBookstore, Amazon Kindle Store, and Barnes and Noble Nook Store. **We also convert speeches, brochures, and almost any other type of literature.**

Frequently Asked Questions

Does it cost anything to submit my manuscript?

It does not cost anything to submit a manuscript. After readying your manuscript, we return a publishing agreement detailing all publishing costs. At that point, you decide if we are to go ahead. If not, you owe nothing.

Do you publish children's books?

Triple J Publishing can publish children's books. Generally, however, because full color pages are used, the costs are higher. If you would like more details, contact us.

How long will it take to produce my book?

Each project is different; thus, **the production time** varies from book to book. Generally, all books are completed within five to six months. This is far less time than is required by the average book publisher. Some seasons are busier than others, influencing production times. Late summer and fall are usually the most hectic. For some authors, completed books are needed by a specific date. If the timeline is less than five months, *Triple J*

Publishing will, upon approval, add a 20% surcharge for all guaranteed delivery date orders. This will be indicated on the agreement form.

Is typesetting included in the printing cost?

For all standard book formats, typesetting is included, provided the manuscript is supplied on CD, USB flash drive, or emailed to *Triple J Publishing*. This will be clearly spelled out in the publishing agreement.

How many words are on a typical typeset page?

The number of words on a page can vary greatly depending on the page layout, typestyle, spacing, and type font size. Typically, 250-450 words per page is an acceptable range.

How many books should I publish?

Generally, unless you have many advance orders and/or do a lot of public speaking, 500 books should be sufficient for a first printing. However, this will have a lot to do with your budget and how well you market your book(s).

How do I copyright my manuscript?

All original works—literary, dramatic, musical, and artistic—are automatically protected under the copyright act, which is universally accepted by most industrialized countries around the world. You do not have to register your copyright to have protection. However, copyrighting your writing provides you with several important rights. With copyright protection, you maintain the right to copy, distribute and license your work. Perhaps most importantly, copyright protection gives you the right to seek financial damages against anyone who violates your rights as the copyright holder. Only by filing for copyright protection for your book, story, poem or screenplay through the US Copyright Office will you secure the right to seek financial damages. It is the author's responsibility to monitor and take legal action in the event of a violation.

Triple J Publishing lists the copyright in the author's name; thus, he or she retains all rights.

How do I type the copyright symbol?

To type the copyright symbol in most word processors, simply place a lowercase "c" between parenthesis (c). Most word processor programs, such as Microsoft Word or Apple's Pages will automatically turn this into the appropriate copyright symbol, ©.

In Windows, you can also hold down the "Alt" key while typing in 0-1-6-9. This will also create the copyright symbol in your text.

What is a mechanical edit?

The purpose of mechanical editing is to prepare an already well structured manuscript for publication. A mechanical edit may address any of the following as needed:

- Correct errors in spelling
- Correct errors in subject/verb agreement
- Correct errors in punctuation
- Identify basic language usage
- Suggest changes when a word is overused

What is a substantive edit?

This level of editing is recommended for manuscripts needing attention to organization, presentation, and sentence structure to clarify meaning and smooth the flow of the text. A substantive edit may address any of the following as needed:

- Suggest improvements to the organization and presentation of material to enhance the reader's experience with the content.

- Suggest recommendations for recasting figures, tables, or charts
- Suggest recommendations to add or delete sections of the manuscript
- Flag terms or phases that may convey an unintended meaning: (bias, negative or offensive tone)
- Identify inconsistencies or contradictions within the text

What is a comprehensive edit?

Triple J Publishing's comprehensive editing process involves recommendations made to a manuscript requiring more extensive structural, organizational, and developmental work. Later stages of editing in this process provide more detailed assistance with the presentation of content as well as the writing mechanics.

Phase 1 – Sample Comprehensive Edit

- Editor reviews entire manuscript, creates a ten page sample edit, and provides the author with a brief overview of the recommended structural and developmental changes.
- Author reviews sample edit to ensure the initial recommendations are consistent with his/her goals.

- Author returns the sample edit, including any additional information or instructions to the editor.
- Author and editor hold a phone conference to discuss the focus of the edit.

Phase 2 – Comprehensive Editing

- Based on the sample edit and the phone conference, the editor continues providing structural, organizational, and developmental recommendations throughout the manuscript.
- Author reviews the edited manuscript, and revises the manuscript based on the editor's recommendations.
- Author returns the revised manuscript.

How can I be sure there are no more errors?

You can't really. No editor will find every error: that's just a fact of life.

How much should I charge for my book?

Usually, you want to price your book competitively with similar books. This may be a price range of $10-$25. From a profit perspective, you should price your book at two to five times the book's cost. (If you plan to sell through bookstores, the retail price should be at least three times the cost.)

When converting my book for an eReader, what formats are used?

Triple J Publishing will convert your files to the following formats: ePUB, .mobi, and PDF. These three formats will allow your book to be read on almost any device.

On what devices will my book be able to be read?

The five main devices on which your can be book read: Apple iPad, Amazon Kindle, Barnes and Noble Nook, Sony eReader and most Tablets. Because many other devices, such as mobile phones, use PDF and ePUB formats for digital books, your book will be available on almost every device.

Is my digital book protected from privacy?

Yes, *Triple J Publishing* uses the Digital Rights Management (DRM) format whenever possible to protect your book's privacy.

Layout for Children's Book

Z is for Zebra.

I am a

dancing zebra

I love to kick up my heels when I am running and playing on the farm.

Cover Design Samples

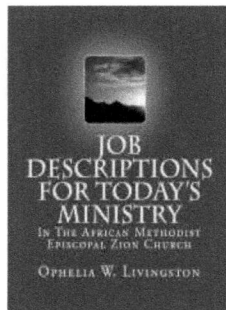

Page Layout Sample 1
Typeface: Eras Medium ITC, Font Size: 13

Grammatical Reference Section

Final typesetting and page layout will usually be done by *Triple J Publishing*. Careful observance of the following guidelines, however, will save considerable extra time and expense in preparing your manuscript for publication.

J. Manuscript Submission
Manuscripts should be submitted in the following formats. Sending an electronic copy is highly recommended.

4. Computer Disk (CD)
   a. CD in any major word processor or page layout program. PDF format is preferred. However, WordPerfect, Microsoft Word, or Microsoft Works, etc. is acceptable. Send TWO identical copies of each CD to minimize disk errors.

Page Layout Sample 2
Typeface: Times New Roman, Font Size 12

The First Church Organization

A church is a very special and unique creation. A "church" is considered a fellowship, which is one of the six core purposes of a church. Fellowship is gathering together as a church and uniting with other believers to encourage one another in faith. Church services, events, meals, small groups, classes and trips are all a part of fellowship. The other five purposes of a church include:

- Discipleship – Following Jesus, learning more about Jesus and the Bible
- Evangelism – Obeying God's command to love and serve unsaved neighbors
- Ministry – Serving others, sharing Christ's love, meeting needs, and teaching
- Prayer – Sincere conversations with God: alone, silent, aloud, in groups or in meetings
- Worship – Believers giving honor, glory and devotion to God

Page Layout Sample 3
Typeface: Veljovik, Font Size: 11

I got a job right away as a physical education teacher at Glendale Elementary. My girlfriend, Beverly, worked as a P.E. teacher as well, across town at the junior high. She was also a physical education major at the same college with Sissy and me.

Sissy was still working part-time in Raleigh and saving as much money as she could. In the fall, she entered Carolina Central in Durham. She didn't stop that education stuff until she'd become a lawyer in Raleigh and headed her own firm. She and her son lived a happy life and came to visit often. She never once mentioned her mother, Mr. Paul, or any of those bad times—and none of them ever came looking for her.

As the years passed, Beverly and I got married and moved into a nice apartment near downtown Glendale. I couldn't go too far from Mama, Grandma Shirl and, of course, my little buddy Jay who, by the time he was thirteen, was extremely talented in basketball. He was a starter on his junior high school's basketball team, and we never missed any of his games even if it meant we had to drive forty miles. Sometimes we even followed him out of state.

Page Layout Sample 4
Typeface: Goudy Old Style, Font Size: 12

I got a job right away as a physical education teacher at Glendale Elementary. My girlfriend, Beverly, worked as a P.E. teacher as well, across town at the junior high. She was also a physical education major at the same college with Sissy and me.

Sissy was still working part-time in Raleigh and saving as much money as she could. In the fall, she entered Carolina Central in Durham. She didn't stop that education stuff until she'd become a lawyer in Raleigh and headed her own firm. She and her son lived a happy life and came to visit often. She never once mentioned her mother, Mr. Paul, or any of those bad times—and none of them ever came looking for her.

As the years passed, Beverly and I got married and moved into a nice apartment near downtown Glendale. I couldn't go too far from Mama, Grandma Shirl and, of course, my little buddy Jay who, by the time he was thirteen, was extremely talented in basketball. He was a starter on his junior high school's basketball team, and we never missed any of his games even if it meant we had to drive forty miles. Sometimes we even followed him out of state.

Page Layout Sample 5
Typeface: Baskerville Old Face, Font Size 12

I got a job right away as a physical education teacher at Glendale Elementary. My girlfriend, Beverly, worked as a P.E. teacher as well, across town at the junior high. She was also a physical education major at the same college with Sissy and me.

Sissy was still working part-time in Raleigh and saving as much money as she could. In the fall, she entered Carolina Central in Durham. She didn't stop that education stuff until she'd become a lawyer in Raleigh and headed her own firm. She and her son lived a happy life and came to visit often. She never once mentioned her mother, Mr. Paul, or any of those bad times—and none of them ever came looking for her.

As the years passed, Beverly and I got married and moved into a nice apartment near downtown Glendale. I couldn't go too far from Mama, Grandma Shirl and, of course, my little buddy Jay who, by the time he was thirteen, was extremely talented in basketball. He was a starter on his junior high school's basketball team, and we never missed any of his games even if it meant we had to drive forty miles. Sometimes we even followed him out of state.

Page Layout Sample 6
Typeface: Times New Roman (Large Print), Font Size:18

I got a job right away as a physical education teacher at Glendale Elementary. My girl-friend, Beverly, worked as a P.E. teacher as well, across town at the junior high. She was also a physical education major at the same college with Sissy and me.

Sissy was still working part-time in Raleigh and saving as much money as she could. In the fall, she entered Carolina Central in Durham. She didn't stop that education stuff until she'd become a lawyer in Raleigh and headed her own firm. She and her son lived a happy life and came to visit often. She never once mentioned her mother, Mr. Paul, or any of those bad times—and none of them ever came looking for her.

As the years passed, Beverly and I got married and moved into a nice apartment near downtown Glendale. I couldn't go too far from Mama, Grandma Shirl and, of course, my little buddy Jay who, by the time he was thirteen, was extremely talented in basketball. He was a starter on his junior high school's basketball team, and we never missed any of his games even if it meant we had to drive forty miles. Sometimes we even followed him out of state.

Page Layout Sample 7

Typeface: Century Schoolbook, Font Size: 11

Week 36– Psalms 22:3

Praise God Because He Inhabits The Praises Of His People

"But thou art holy, O thou that inhabitest the praises of Israel."

Perhaps you have heard your Worship Leader in your church proclaim that God inhabits the praises of His people. This is one of God's principle works. This means that praising God brings you to His presence and power. What better way to illustrate this truth than through the story of Paul and Silas in Acts 16.

Both were arrested, severely beaten and imprisoned. One might think praying and praising God would have been the last thing Paul and Silas would have considered doing. But that was exactly what they did! Suddenly, there was an earthquake. The prison doors swung wide open and Paul, Silas and all the other prisoners were released from their bondage. Their **praises** unleashed the mighty power of God.

Musical Selections:

Gospel: "Lift Your Head"

Hymn: "Praise Him"

Prayer:

I will always praise You for who You are and what You have done for me in my life. Amen.

Before you send in your manuscript, be sure to include:

❑ Complete manuscript on your CD or USB flash drive (softcopy).

❑ Complete manuscript on paper (hardcopy).

❑ Mail-in checklist form or online checklist, including your email address or physical address for courier delivery or email delivery of book (proofs and/or cover design proofs).

❑ Bibliography, any endnotes (complete with publishing information, page numbers for quotations)

❑ Dedication, acknowledgement, forward, introduction, testimonials, preface, about the author, etc, (if desired in finished book)

❑ Table of contents

❑ Figures, tables, charts, graphs, art, photos, etc. must be identified.

Mail-in Checklist Form

Clip this form and send it with your manuscript to:

Triple J Publishing
150 N. Steele Street, Suite 102
Sanford, NC 27330
or
E-mail: triplejpublishing@gmail.com

(Print clearly and include your street address)

Name: _____

Address: _____

_____

Home Phone: _____

Mobile Number: _____

Fax # (if available) _____

Email: _____

I am planning to use the following: (indicate number)
❑ Photos _____
❑ Indices _____
❑ Charts/Graphs _____
Line art/drawings _____

I anticipate my manuscript will require:
❑ Proofreading
❑ Major editing

51

❑ Minor editing
❑ No additional editing

The enclosed disk or flash drive is in the following format
❑ Microsoft Word
❑ Microsoft Works
❑ PDF
❑ WordPerfect

The level of cover design I am considering is:
❑ Gold ($700)
❑ Silver ($550)
❑ Bronze ($450)

I want my interior page color to be:
❑ White
❑ Cream (higher cost)

I want my interior pictures, charts, drawing, art, etc. to be:
❑ Black/White
❑ Color

Mail-in Checklist Form

Clip this form and send it with your manuscript to:

Triple J Publishing
150 N. Steele Street, Suite 102
Sanford, NC 27330

or

E-mail: triplejpublishing@gmail.com

(Print clearly and include your street address)

Name: _____

Address: _____

_____

Home Phone: _____

Mobile Number: _____

Fax # (if available) _____

Email: _____

I am planning to use the following: (indicate number)
- ❑ Photos _____
- ❑ Indices _____
- ❑ Charts/Graphs _____
- ❑ Line art/drawings _____

I anticipate my manuscript will require:
- ❑ Proofreading
- ❑ Major editing

❑ Minor editing
❑ No additional editing

The enclosed disk or flash drive is in the following format
❑ Microsoft Word
❑ Microsoft Works
❑ PDF
❑ WordPerfect

The level of cover design I am considering is:
❑ Gold ($700)
❑ Silver ($550)
❑ Bronze ($450)

I want my interior page color to be:
❑ White
❑ Cream (higher cost)

I want my interior pictures, charts, drawing, art, etc. to be:
❑ Black/White
❑ Color

www.ingramcontent.com/pod-product-compliance
Lightning Source LLC
Chambersburg PA
CBHW051047030426
42339CB00006B/237